SELF-PUBLISHING BOOKS FOR PASSIVE INCOME

STEP BY STEP GUIDE TO SELF-PUBLISHING BOOKS FOR COMPLETE BEGINNERS.

CHARLIE NEWMAN

To my Father, Mother, and My Guide

to whom I shall remain indebted

for setting the foundation on which

all my books are inspired.

Contents

Contents

CHAPTER ONE

Introduction

Making money through passive income is everyone's dream, and if you are one of them, then this book is for you. In passive income, you create the resources once and make money from them for months to years without interfering.

There are many ways through which you can generate passive income. For example, blogging, book publishing, mobile application development, royalty for designs, print on demand, selling your art, etc.

This book covers one such source, called book publishing. Book publishing is a process where you write or create a book and then publish it for commercial sale.

There are three ways to publish a book.

- by sub-contracting your book to any publication house for publishing (the traditional way of book publishing).
- You can publish your book on your own.
- You can self-publish your books through self-publishing platforms like Amazon, Draft2Digital, etc.

All three have their merits and demerits.

You make the maximum profit when you publish your book on your own. But here is the catch. With your own book publishing, you may have to market and sell the book for yourself, which is definitely not an easy task. Also, you have to take care of technical things like editing your book, running a publication, buying an ISBN, copyright-related issues, etc.

Often, with sub-contracting, authors make less money, and the maximum portion of book profit will be retained by these publishers for marketing and distribution purposes. The advantage of this process is that your publisher will take care of all the heavy lifting jargon like book editing, the publishing process, copyright-related issues, marketing and sales of your book, etc. These are the reasons why they pay very little to the author.

As compared to both the options above, publishing books through self-publishing platforms is like a middle path. Where self-publishing platforms provide a platform for both authors to publish the books and buyers to buy the books, Here, the author has to edit and publish his book on his own, and he has to take care of copyright-related stuff too. In return, these platforms provide a free ISBN for each book you publish, and they advertise your book to their audience for free. They often take a commission per book per sale. They typically charge 70% to 60% commission, which is significantly lower than third-party publishing houses.

Recently, publishing books through a self-publishing platform has skyrocketed because of its simplicity and time to market. It creates a win-win opportunity for the platform, for the authors as well as for the buyers. Often, all three will get a fair price for their work. (Debatable though).

Also, nowadays, publishing books on a self-publishing platform is completely free with zero starting cost.

In this book, I will cover how you can use this opportunity to make money. Here I will cover the basics of self-publishing, steps to publishing your first book, and converting this book publishing into a full-scale business.

In this book, I will cover book publishing through self-publishing platforms. I will use the terms "book publishing" and "self-publishing" interchangeably; they mean the same.

CHAPTER TWO

Why is Self-Publishing the best Business?

Book publishing is the most viable form of passive income generation business because, often, you have to write and publish a book once, and once sales start, from that point on, you will be making money till the end of the life of that book.

Points supporting the above statement:

- Initial capital to start self-publishing is zero on almost all platforms. So, to start, all you need is a laptop, word pad, or colour pad and a little bit of creativity. That's all you need.
- Often, once books start to get popular, they will keep on selling for years without much change from your side.
- All the tools to start a self-publishing business and write and publish your book are completely free. For example, to write a high-content book (HCB), like a self-help book, all you need is Microsoft Word. For the book cover design, you can use the free version of Canva.com, and for publishing a book, you can use a free self-publishing account.
- Also, you will get lots of free ideas on Google and YouTube for your topic, and the best part is that basic training for publishing books is also freely available on YouTube. All you have to invest in is time, patience, and commitment. Tell me what else you

need.

- Your books will be sold all over the world, 24 x 7 a year. This increases your chance to make more money and for a longer time.
- Still, self-publishing is a less crowded field as of 2021, so you still have plenty of time to start and make money for years.
- Self-publishing platforms often do not delay your royalty, and they have a history of paying your royalty on time and with complete transparency.
- There are thousands of niches in the book publishing domain, so you will never run out of ideas and niches.
- With hard work and good luck, many make over $100k per month in this business. This business has some serious money. So, take this business very seriously.

CHAPTER THREE

How Passive is the Self-Publishing Business?

To qualify as a true passive income business, one must follow the principle of creating once and forgetting.

Let me tell you the truth: the self-publishing business is almost a passive income business, and it is not 100% passive business, and here are some points supporting it.

- Every book has an end of life. Some may have 2 to 5 years, some may have more than 30 years, and some may have less than 1 year. It all depends on the niche and market response. That is why, for continuous and consistent income, you may have to keep on adding books to your store.
- Books' content often gets outdated, so you must keep on updating the books by releasing updated versions then and there to keep them relevant to current market demand.
- With time, competition will also increase, and profit margins will go down. So, you must keep on adding new content and also keep on marketing to keep your book visible to the audience.
- Self-publishing platforms change policies often, and this may impact your book's sale (if your book falls into such a category). So, you must keep on monitoring such changes, and if required, you may have to make changes to your book and re-publish it.
- Often, the self-publishing business model gets updated with new ways to publish books. which can shift your income from the

existing model to the new model. For example, with the introduction of audiobooks, part of the sale has shifted from eBooks and printed books to audiobooks. So, you must also update your book to reflect such business models to maintain your passive income.

These are some of the important reasons why you have to work back and forth between self-publishing businesses. 100% passive income is a myth.

CHAPTER FOUR

Benefits of Self-Publishing Business

- Self-publishing has provided many authors an opportunity to publish their books and showcase their talent without much hassle, which was very difficult in the traditional publishing days. Back then, traditional book publishers often only published books by famous authors or authors with very strong educational backgrounds. Those with an average education but strong writing skills used to have a difficult time finding a publisher for their book, and they frequently end up paying thousands of dollars upfront to bring their book to market.
- In traditional book publishing, you have to publish a minimum number of books to reduce printing costs. which was a big risk for many publishers as well as for authors. Often, the minimum book quantity was 500 to 5000 in some cases. But with self-publishing, because of technological advancement and optimised printing techniques, book printing is now an on-demand-based business. This reduces the requirement of putting up huge amounts of upfront money, both for authors and publishers.
- Self-publishing opportunities have turned many newbie writers into successful authors.
- The self-publishing opportunity has also contributed to many new niches and many new books for worldwide readers to enjoy.

- The online e-commerce platform of self-publishing companies has reduced the distance between the countries, and with a fingertip, one can purchase the books written by the author, who is sitting thousands of miles away.
- Self-publishing businesses have provided employment and entrepreneurial opportunity for millions of people.
- The earning potential of the self-publishing business is enormous; many people have achieved an average monthly income of $100,000.
- In contrast to traditional publishing, authors own the full rights to their published books in self-publishing, and they can control their pricing as well as when to publish and unpublish the book.
- The self-publishing business is completely driven by digital technology, and everything happens online, including payments.
- With the introduction of eBooks and audiobooks, self-publishing is moving towards low carbon print and green business solutions.
- Self-publishing gives an opportunity to authors with a lack of funding to start their publishing business free of cost.

The way the self-publishing business is growing, we can see that, in coming years, book publishing through self-publishing platforms will become the industry standard.

Till now, I have tried to cover the basics of the self-publishing business. I hope you got a basic understanding of the self-publishing environment and how it works. In the next section, I will cover how to publish your first book and more.

CHAPTER FIVE

Book Publishing Categories

Book publishing is broadly divided into 3 categories:

- Based on Niche.
- Based on the Book Format
- based on language.

Let us study each of the above in detail.

CHAPTER SIX

Niche-Based Book Publishing

Based on niche, book publishing is divided into 3 main categories:

- NCB (No Content Book)
- Low Content Book (LCB)
- HCB stands for High Content Book.

No Content Book (NCB) Publishing:

No Content Books have very little written content in them. It does not mean it is completely blank. The NCB content is often in the form of lines, blank boxes, or blank pages with borders, etc.

These books have very little usage of words like copy-right statements, headings, author info, etc. But the main content is almost blank or of very simple format.

Some examples of NCB are:

- Blank Journal
- lined journal.

- Composition notebook
- Blank colouring books.
- Blank comic books.
- blank-page book, etc.

The advantages of No Content Book (NCB) publishing:

- NCB is often very easy and simple to design.
- In most cases, free tools are enough to design and publish NCB books.
- Often, beginners are advised to start their book publishing journey with this category.
- If you are in the right niche, you can easily make a couple of dollars per month from NCB.
- NCBs are often consumable goods. So, their demand will never come down.
- You do not have to worry about competition since NCB has thousands of sub-niches for publishing books and you are only limited by your imagination.
- NCB helps beginners easily understand the book publishing business and process.
- In NCB, the time to market is very small. You can publish your first book in a day or a half.
- Capital investment in NCB is zero to a negligible amount.

The following are the limitations of No Content Book (NCB) publishing:

- Because of the low time to market and being beginner-friendly, competition is very high in NCB. Competition is sky-high.

- Nowadays, succeeding in NCB requires you to do deep keyword research and heavy marketing.
- With NCB, you will be limited to the printed version of the book only. You cannot sell NCB in the form of an eBook or audiobook.
- Since competition is very high, chances of getting copy-right claims too are very high.
- NCB's success not only depends on the quality of the book but also on the number of books you upload.

Despite many disadvantages, I suggest you start with this category to better understand the book publishing business and process.

Here are some suggested sub-niches for No Content Book Publishing:

- Plain Blank Journals or Notebooks
- Plain Line Journals or Notebooks
- Calligraphy Practice Papers and Books
- Dot Grid Notebook/Journal.
- Notebook for Guitar Tabs
- Graph notebook
- Blank Sketch Book
- Notebook on Graph Paper
- Kanji Practice Notebook
- The Primary Story Journal
- Blank Comic Book
- Cursive handwriting books, etc.

NCB Publishing's Earning Capacity:

With the good number of books in the store, on average, you can expect an income in the range of $100 to $2000 per month.

Low Content Book (LCB) Publishing:

The low-content book contains enough words to give it some meaningful content but not enough to make it a full-scale regular book. Low content books (LCB) fall between NCB and HCB. For example, 100 questions for couples is an ideal example of LCB where it contains 1 question per page and space for response.

The fundamental theory behind the low-content book is to engage the book buyer in some kind of activity rather than just keeping them busy reading the book.

Some examples of Low-Content Books are:

- Kids' Maths Activity Book
- guest entry book.
- music composition books.
- Tell me about your story journals, Mom.
- truck drivers' log journals, etc.
- all kinds of activity and game books

The Benefits of Low-Content Book Publishing:

- The profit margin in the low-content book is far more than NCB.
- LCB has 1000's of sub-niches to publish books into. You will never run out of opportunities and ideas.
- Successful LCB publishers make more than $100,000 per month from LCB.
- There are plenty of free tools available out there for designing LCBs.

- LCB provides an opportunity to build the brand.
- LCB is beginner-friendly. Since you don't have to worry much about language and grammar,
- Many people have created their careers out of LCB publishing.
- LCB has a much shorter time to market than HCB but a little longer than NCB.
- LCB does not work on the concept of quantity like NCB. If you have a handful of quality books in the right niche, then you can easily make 500 to 3000 dollars per month in passive income.
- Capital investment in LCB is very low, and if you can manage to create content on your own, then capital is almost zero.

The Limitations of Low-Content Book Publishing:

- Because of competition, most of the LCB niches are saturated. Because of reasons like very good money with the opportunity to replace your full-time income; passive income opportunity; work from anywhere opportunity; and popularity, the book publishing business has skyrocketed and, because of that, many have entered LCB, NCB, and HCB and started publishing thousands of books in all possible niches every day.
- Because of competition, the LCB business needs aggressive marketing and demands handsome capital to be invested in.
- The content in the LCB must be of high quality. Often, high-quality content requires both capital and time to be invested.
- Unlike NCB, LCB publishing needs creativity, quality, and patience to succeed in this business.
- Most of the LCB niches are often seasonal. And hence, your earnings will also be seasonal. For example, Father's Day journal, Christmas journal, etc.
- Copyright claims are often the biggest challenge in LCB. If not taken care of in advance, it may result in the banning of your self-publishing account permanently, and also you may have to

face legal action from the concerned authority.

Here are some suggested sub-niches for Low-Content Book Publishing:

- Festival books and journals.
- Activity Books—Kids, adults, etc.
- Colouring Books for Adults and Children
- Quotation Books
- Planners
- games and puzzle books.
- Journals.
- Log Books—Guest, Travel, Fuel, Diet, etc.
- Blank Recipe/Cookbook
- Kid's Learning Book
- Prompts: notebooks
- autograph books, etc.

LCB has thousands of sub-niches that are highly difficult to cover here. I have covered the most active and famous sub-niches. You can check out my SELF-PUBLISHING NICHE IDEAS BOOK for more details.

LCB Publishing's Earning Capacity:

On average, one can earn $500 to $50,000 per month with quality books covering a wide variety of sub-niches and with good marketing strategy. The LCB business has a huge market and great earning potential.

High Content Book (HCB) Publishing:

High-content books are those which have high word content and very little to zero activity-related stuff. Normally, a word count of 1500 or more is termed a high-content book (though it is not a strict rule but just a rule of thumb).

Examples of high-content books are everywhere. From school, to college, to degree textbooks, novels, motivational books, stories, etc.

High-content books are subdivided into the following categories:

- Short Reads (15 to 45 minutes of reading time)
- Medium Reads (Reading time: 45 minutes to 2 hours)
- Longer reads (over 2 hours)

The Advantages of High Content Book (HCB) Publishing:

- The high-content book provides a huge opportunity to build the author's authority and brand.
- The end of life for HCB is very high. Some of the most famous books written 30 to 40 years ago are still selling without much change in the content.
- HCB has the highest earning potential when compared to NCB and LCB. Because HCB can be published in many formats, like eBooks, printed books, and audiobooks,
- HCB is the highway to popularity. Many times, books that have a high popularity tag will also get celebrity status for their authors.
- HCB provides an opportunity to convert your book into movies, TV shows, etc., and provides one more stream of income.

- The high-content book can be published in multiple formats as compared to the LCB and NCB.
- HCB does not need complex skills like graphic design and editing. All you need is a good command of the language in which you are writing the book.
- The tools for publishing HCB are completely free. You just need Microsoft Word and a free account with Grammarly.
- You can charge a high price for HCB as compared to LCB and NCB.
- According to my experience, HCB is the true source of passive income as compared to LCB and NCB.

The Limitations of High Content Book (HCB) Publishing:

- The time to market is often very high as compared to LCB and NCB.
- Your command of the language in which you are publishing the book has to be very good.
- Since HCB is not consumable like NCB or LCB, its sales will be lower as compared to other categories.
- Book copyright theft is the biggest problem for HCB. Many times, in smaller cities, we can find a duplicate copy of the famous books being sold for a very cheap price, which can hurt your sales to a greater extent.
- Resale and renting of the books are also the biggest problems for HCB publishers. Many times, people read the book and resell it within their circle to save money.
- HCB needs high starting capital. Though for simple books you don't need money, for serious books you may have to invest in cover design, book editing, proofreading, audiobook conversion, etc. (you may need around $500 to $1000 for well-published books).

Here are some suggested sub-niches for High Content Book (HCB) Publishing:

- Novels: Romance, Suspense, Crime, etc.
- Self-help: Motivation, Anger Management, etc.
- Health and Fitness: Keto Diet, Healthy Habits, etc.
- Children's Books – Comics, Story Books, etc.
- Lifestyle: Travel, food, fashion, etc.
- Sports.
- History.
- Technical.
- Business and Economics, etc.

As I stated before, all these LCB, NCB, and HCB have thousands of niches, which makes it difficult to mention here.

HCB Publishing's Earning Capacity:

The best part of HCB is that you can publish the same book in multiple formats, like eBook, printed book, and audiobook. And each one of them will be sold separately, independently of each other. which gives a huge boost to your earning potential.

Also, many high-content books are turned into movies like Harry Potter, TV Series, Short Films, etc., which can generate a huge royalty amount for the author.

Building an author authority figure can bring many earning opportunities, like penning your opinion for other books, being a guest of honour at many functions, selling personally signed copies at a higher price, etc.

On average, HCB publishing can make you from $500 to $50,000 or more per month.

HCB publishing is not only about publishing a book but also about building an author's authority and popularity. HCB is a completely different game as compared to LCB and NCB.

CHAPTER SEVEN

Book Publishing Based on the Book Format

Based on the book format, the self-publishing business is divided into 3 broad categories.

- Digital Book Publishing (formats like eBook, PDF, etc.).
- Printed Book Publishing (Paperback, Hardcover, Spiral Binding, etc.)
- Audio book.

Digital Format Books (eBooks, PDF's, and other softcopy books):

After the computer and internet boom, digital goods and services started finding space in everyday life. One such digital product is digital format books.

Digital books are also called eBooks or "Soft Books." (no physical format, only digital format) are the most famous and easiest to produce.

Many self-publishing platforms provide space to host and sell your eBooks in their store. The most famous among them is the Amazon Kindle eBook store. Amazon also provides eBook readers like Kindle eReaders to help customers consume and read eBooks.

eBooks come in many formats, like EPUB, PDF, Doc, MOBI, etc.

Advantages of Digital Format Books:

- easy to access.
- low cost.
- best suited for HCBs.
- It sells easily as compared to a printed book or audio book.
- It's easy to store and carry. You can read the books on your personal computer or on the go on your mobile phone.
- It is best suited for quick access to books.
- You can sell eBooks not only on self-publishing platforms but also on your websites as downloadable resources.
- You can adjust the font based on your preference while reading, which is not possible in the printed version of the book.
- The reach of eBooks is far greater and easier than that of printed books. Because to buy an eBook, all you need is a smartphone.
- Digital books are environment-friendly. You do not have to cut trees for eBooks. We can say that the carbon footprint for publishing and consuming eBooks is far less than the traditional paperback.

The Disadvantages of Books in Digital Format:

- The profit margin is very low as compared to audio and printed books.
- Often, soft copies of books are susceptible to hacking.
- Still, most of the world's population is not used to eBooks. They still prefer printed copies.
- LCB and NCB books cannot be sold as eBooks.

- eBooks are not consumable, so once a book is sold, it will be available in the same condition for years.

Printed Books (Paperback, Spiralbound, Hardcover, etc.):

We are all aware of printed books because that is what was first introduced to the world as a book format. A printed copy is perhaps the most suited for the maximum age group around the world. Despite the technological updates, people still prefer printed copies of the book for many reasons.

Printed books can be divided into 3 main categories:

- Paperback books (Priced low and sells well)
- Hardcover books (Highly priced and less preferred)
- Spiral bound books (priced high & applicable to specific niches)

There is nothing much to explain in these formats as they are self-explanatory. What I suggest is to go first with a paperback book, and once the book is popular, only think about hardcover. Because the average book reader mostly prefers paperbacks as compared to hardcovers for many reasons, for example:

- Paperback books are flexible and easy to carry in bags and in pockets.
- Paperback books are affordable as compared to hardcovers, etc.

Spiral bound books are limited to specific niches like diaries, notebooks, etc.

Benefits of Printed Books:

- Printed books are perhaps the oldest form and also the most preferred format by all age groups, especially the elderly.
- E-books require you to be digitally friendly. But unfortunately, most of the world's population is not that digitally literate.
- We can easily sit and read printed books for hours. But the same is not true for digital books and audiobooks.
- Printed books are eye-friendly.
- Gifting printed books is far easier than gifting audiobooks and eBooks.
- Note-making and bookmarking are far easier in a printed book than in an eBook.
- You can easily resell printed books rather than audio or eBooks.
- Profit margins are higher in printed books than in eBooks.
- Printed books are consumable products. They have an end of life. For example, usually the book's paper quality will deteriorate over time, and people will often buy the same book again and again.
- We can publish LCB, NCB, and HCB in printed format, which is not possible in eBooks and audiobooks. eBooks and audiobooks only support HCB.

Disadvantages of Printed Books include:

- It is more expensive than eBooks.
- The reach of the paperback is far less than the eBook in many countries.
- One printed book can be used by many individuals, which impacts the sale.

- Relative to eBooks, printed books are often sold less in HCB niches (debatable).
- For LCB and NCB, only paperback and spiral bound options are available. which reduces its market reach and profit margin.
- Printed books are not eco-friendly. You need to cut trees to print books. (I am a nature lover and suggest you stick to eBooks wherever possible).
- You need a high capital investment in printed books as compared to eBooks.

Audiobooks:

Audiobooks have recently been introduced on many self-publishing platforms like Amazon, Apple, etc.

High Content Audiobooks are abridged versions of High Content Books that are read aloud.

Using ACX is the best way to publish your audiobook to Audible.

The Advantages of Audio Books:

- The profit margin in audiobooks is high as compared to digital books and printed books.
- Audiobooks are best suited for people who love to listen rather than read books.
- You can listen to audiobooks while driving (though that is not the best time to listen), while doing exercise, traveling, or doing any work.
- Often, audiobook content is conveyed better than printed or digital books.
- You can add voice modulation and expression in audiobooks to add more value to the book's content, which is highly impossible

in other formats.

- Because the audio format is not consumable, it will last for a long time.
- This format is also suitable for illiterates, blind people, and elderly people who cannot read for some reason.
- Audiobooks right now have very little competition as compared to other formats.

Disadvantages of the Audio Book Format:

- You have to put up a lot of capital to produce good-quality audiobooks. (at least $500 to $1000). And this is the biggest setback for many beginners. What I suggest here is first start with eBooks and printed books, and once you make enough money, invest that into audiobooks.
- Audiobooks are not suited for digitally illiterate people.
- Only HCB books are suited for audio books.
- Still, the audiobook market is not mature yet. So, sales are not up to the mark. But audiobooks have a great future.
- Despite digital literacy, many readers still prefer printed books over digital books or audiobooks.

CHAPTER EIGHT

Book Publishing Based on Language

Based on language, book publishing is categorised in 2 ways:

- Local Language Books.
- Universal Language Books (English).

Local Language Books:

They are more well-known in their respective regions.Most of the books published in the local language are niche-related to art, culture, poetry, etc. Also, many famous books can be converted into local language books based on demand.

The advantages of local language books are:

- They target a very focused market, which increases their chances of selling books.
- Getting recognition for the author is far easier in local language books than in the English language.
- Competition is less in the local language.

Disadvantages of local language books:

- Local language book sales are often very low as compared to English books.
- Market reach is far less in local language books than in English-language books.
- Books are frequently priced lower than English-language books.
- Local language books are limited in niche selection.
- Many self-publishing platforms do not support local language publishing yet.
- Creating and editing local language books is far more difficult than in English.

Universal Language Books (English):

The English language is the most understood and interpreted language in the world. The English language is termed as the global language and the common language for communication between different countries.

Because of globalization, nowadays everyone is learning English as a second language. That's why books published in the English language get good visibility and have a good reach worldwide.

The advantages of English-language books:

- All self-publishing platforms are based on the English language. And they use the English language as their main language of publication.

- You get very good technical support in publishing an English book compared to any local language book.
- Typing in the English language is far easier than the local language. English language books can be designed in any commonly used editor and can be edited easily and in a short amount of time.
- The technical challenges in the book publishing process in the English language are far fewer than in local language books.
- English books are often priced higher than local language books, which increases the profit margin per sale.
- English is a globally recognised and widely practised language. That is why the English book market's reach is far greater than local language books. Therefore, their sales are also high.

English Language Books Have the Following Drawbacks:

- Because of the global language status, competition is very high.
- Still, part of the world's population prefers local language books over books in the English language.
- Local art and culture books should be written in the local language rather than in English.

CHAPTER NINE

Self-Publishing Platforms

Self-publishing platforms provide software platforms for authors and publishers to publish their books on their own. It is like a win-win platform for both self-publishers and self-publishing platforms.

Self-publishing platforms provide traffic for buyers for their books, and they will also take care of the order process like buying, selling, and delivery of books. All you have to do is upload the book as per their standard.

Some famous self-publishing platforms are:

- Amazon KDP–Famous and widely used.
- Draft2Digital
- Lulu
- Smashwords
- Bookbaby
- IngramSpark
- Kobo, etc.

Self-publishing platforms frequently charge 50 to 70 percent of your book's royalties per sale for their services.

Though the commission rate sounds high, it's worth the effort as compared to publishing books through third-party publishers or self-publishing books.

Benefits of self-publishing platforms include:

- They provide a win-win platform for authors and publishers. The biggest problems for authors and publishers are buyers' traffic, international market reach, and delivery. which will be taken care of by the self-publishing platform itself.
- These platforms take care of the purchase and return of your books, and they pay royalty payments consistently too, so you don't have to worry about finances.
- They reduce the time to market drastically. Once you publish your book, it will be visible to buyers all over the world within a couple of minutes to hours.
- Once you publish your book as per their guidelines, then you can peacefully set aside the rest of the bookselling process and continue working on the other books. Once your book is reviewed and live on the market, a self-publishing platform will take over your book and it will do the rest of the marketing and selling on your behalf. Once selling picks up, then your books will keep on selling for years to come and will make you a royalty as a passive income for years.
- You do not have to worry about the marketing of your book; it will be taken care of by a self-publishing platform.
- You can price your book as per your choice with very few conditions.
- You can make frequent changes to your book, like price changes, cover changes, content changes, etc., and all these changes will be visible to buyers within a short time.
- The best part of self-publishing is that you can have full control over the book publishing process and publication dates.
- Any important changes can be made quickly and easily since everything is in digital format.
- This platform provides an opportunity for you to study the buyers' sentiments and, according to that, you can make changes to the book as well as publish new books as needed.

- All the heavy lifting of publishing is taken care of by these platforms for you.
- They also provide a free ISBN for your book, which is a great help for many authors, especially beginners.

Limitations of Self-Publishing platforms:

- You will not have control over royalties and commission rates.
- Many self-publishing platforms do not allow you to upload your books to multiple self-publishing platforms.
- The book promotion and marketing process is not transparent.
- Many times, abiding by self-publishing platform guidelines is very difficult, and because of that, many good authors get banned from these platforms for a lifetime.
- Many times, their marketing process is not enough to bring in sales, and you may have to do the marketing in the form of advertisements on your own.
- These platforms do not guarantee consistent sales.
- These platforms own the rights to your book published in certain cases.
- Self-publishing platforms are often a bit complicated for many authors and beginners to operate.
- They often charge more commission for new publishers.
- Also, recently, royalties are being slowly reduced and the commission rate is kept on increasing because of monopoly, and this is hurting the profit margin of authors.
- You have to maintain and monitor your published books, and they do not provide any assistance in this.

Though there are many challenges in self-publishing your books, the overall advantage that you get is far more than the drawbacks. That's why self-publishing has started booming these days and may soon become the industry standard for publishing books.

CHAPTER TEN

A Step-By-Step Guide to Self-Publishing Your First Book

In this section, I will cover how to publish your first book from end to end. Please note that I will not go deep into how to write a book for HCB or how to select and draw graphics for LCB and NCB. That is your part of the work, but what I will cover is simple and beginner-friendly step-by-step guidelines to publish your first book.

Step 1: Create an Account for Self-Publishing

There are plenty of self-publishing platforms out there which you can utilise to publish your books. Or you can publish the same book on all those platforms. Anything is fine.

But for complete beginners, select one platform which has more buyers' reach. For example, Amazon KDP is a famous and well-established platform for self-publishing books around the world. Its reach is more than 90% as compared to other platforms.

I recommend that you begin publishing through Amazon KDP, as in many cases, the Amazon KDP platform is sufficient to generate passive income as well as to establish a full-scale publishing business.

You need the following items to open your publishing account:

- Valid ID proof.
- Your income tax number
- national bank account in your name. (If you are a minor, then you can use your parent's account number and income tax number.
- mobile number and an email ID for login and other transaction activity.

Important points before opening your self-publishing account:

- If you are already banned from self-publishing platforms, then you cannot re-open or open a new account in your name ever again.
- Do not create multiple accounts. It is against self-publishing platform policy.
- All the documents that you are producing for opening the account should be in your name or in the name of the person for whom you are opening the account.
- Do not provide false information like wrong tax numbers or wrong bank account numbers. Sooner or later, you will be caught and be banned from these platforms for life.

Step 2: Know Yourself in Order to Know Your Business.

Before publishing your first book, ask yourself this question: what is it that you are expecting from this business? You want money, or you want to be a famous author, or do you want both?

Also, ask yourself: are you good at writing HCB books, or are you good at creating artistic content, or are you not good at anything?

If you love writing, then start with the HCB category. You can select many sub-niches like self-motivation books, technical books, short stories and novels, etc.

If you are very good at artistic design and graphics, then start with LCB and create books in sub-niches like colouring books, journals, etc.

And if you are not good at anything, then do not worry. Start with NCB and publish books like a composition notebook, blank line journals, etc. Later on, you can outsource your ideas for creating the book content.

It is also very important for you to understand yourself first. Because many times, people are interested in making money from self-publishing but are not interested in creating content. In those cases, I suggest you outsource your ideas to create the book, and then, once everything is verified, go ahead and publish it in your name or a pen name.

Step 3: Perform Keyword Research

Once you have finalised your broad niches like NCB, LCB, or HCB, you have to dig deep into the specific niches called sub-niches or micro-niches to target your book for a specific audience for better results.

There are many ways through which you can do keyword research. You can do manual keyword research or you can take the help of keyword research tools like Helium 10, Keyword IO, AMZ Suggestion Expander, etc. or even outsource keyword research.

The Best Free and Paid Tools for Keyword Research:

- Amazon search bar itself. (Free).
- Amazon Ads keyword suggestion.
- Other: Print on Demand websites like Redbubble, Etsy, Teespring, etc.
- Google Search bar with chrome extensions like whatsmyserp and/or keywordseverywhere. (There are both free and paid versions.)
- Google Trends can be used to check keyword trends.
- Publisher Rocket (Paid).
- KDSpy (Paid).
- Keyword Spy.
- Kindle Samurai (Paid)
- Helium-10 (Paid)
- Bookbaby.
- SpyFu.

The Best Free and Paid Chrome Extensions for Keyword Research.

- AMZ Suggestion Expander Chrome Plugin (Free).
- DS Amazon Quick View for BSR Monitor (Free).
- Amazon product data from Jungle Scout.
- AMZScout Pro is a product research and FBA calculator for Amazon.
- SellerApp—Amazon product and keyword research.
- Helium 10 is an all-purpose Amazon KDP Research tool.

- Keepa—Amazon price tracker.
- The Camelizer is an Amazon price tracker.
- AMZ Base: Amazon product research
- AmazeOwl - A powerful product search engine.

The Best Approach for Keyword Research

- If you are a beginner, then I suggest you start with manual keyword research to understand the entire process. Many times, paid tools will not effectively suggest the best keywords. And it is observed that manual keyword research, in most cases, produces excellent results.
- While doing keyword research, search for those keywords (niches) that have suggested books with a BSR (Best Seller Rank) of less than 300K and Amazon search results with less than 1000 searches.
- You can also conduct competitor research. Note down the primary keywords for which your competitors' books are ranking on page 1.
- List keywords (short tail and long tail) separately for creating titles and sub-titles.
- Make a list of semantic keywords for secondary keywords.
- For one main targeted keyword, there can be many long-tail keywords, and each one of the long-tail keywords will act as a sub-niche for that keyword.
- If you do not know any keywords to start with, start researching best sellers in the Amazon books category. You can note down repeated keywords on page 1 for multiple sections, and from there you can start your research. For example, in a best seller, if you see many books with "habit" in their title or sub-title, then habit is the primary keyword and from there you can start the sub-niche keyword research and figure out long-tail keywords like "30 Day Habit Challenge," "How to develop healthy habits

that last a long time," etc.

- Understand that keyword research is not as easy as it sounds, and this process can take from a few hours to many days to finalise possible best-selling keywords. So, please have patience.
- Book publishing is not a get-rich scheme where you publish some random books and you start to make money. It is a full-scale business, and you have to approach it like a business.
- While doing keyword research, also research about book size, and book language. Find out which book size sells best for which niche and which language is best suited for which niche. For example, 8.5 x 11 inch book size is best suited for LCB and NCB books in many sub-niches like colouring books, kids' activity books, etc., and 6 x 9 inches is best suited for HCB self-help books. And if you are writing a language learning book like Russian to Japanese, then targeting that book for other languages and countries is often not that useful.So, keep these in mind while doing keyword research.
- We approach keyword research in two ways. One for narrowing down niches and sub-niches, Second, for title, sub-title, and additional keywords.
- Niche and sub-niches are often short-tail and long-tail keywords.
- The title should contain your main targeting keyword, and the sub-title can include supporting keywords with any more information as required.
- Supporting keywords are often semantic search keywords for your main keywords.
- Find out keywords with high profitability.

You can follow a simple formula:

> "*High Demand (BSR) + Low Competition (Search Volume) = Best Keyword.*"

Lorose

Simple keyword research steps to remember

- Finalize the targeting keyword.
- Finalize Book Size.
- Finalize Book Language.
- Finalize bool length (page length).
- Finalize the title and sub-title.
- Write a description.
- Complete 7 semantic keywords for the sub-title and supporting keywords sections in platforms such as Amazon.

Here are some of the all-time best-selling and evergreen niches for you:

- Self-help,
- Business and Money
- Health, Fitness, and Dieting
- Activity Books, etc.

Expected outcome of the keyword research process:

When you complete the keyword research, you should have finalised the following points:

- You should shortlist the main targeting keyword under which you will publish your book. For example, "Valentine's Day Gift". Remember, the targeted keyword is what book buyers will be typing in the search bar to search for the book.
- You must come up with a specific niche where you want to publish your book. The researched niche should be something like "Valentine's Day gift ideas for wife."

- You should have shortlisted book size, page length, etc.
- title and sub-title. (Your target keyword must be included in the title, and any other keywords related to the target keyword must be included in the sub-title.)
- 7 semantic keywords that support your targeted keyword
- List out different sources (like competitors' books, table of content, some reference websites, and some YouTube videos around that targeted keyword) for creating book interiors or content.
- Book Description
- author name that you may like, which should not clash with other author names.

These are the things you should finalise before starting the book writing process.

Step 4: Create Book Content.

Once you finalise the niche, it's time for you to create the content of the book.

You can either create the content on your own if you do not have the budget, or you can hire ghostwriters or graphic designers to create the book content for you.

Creating book content for yourself is up to you and depends on your skills and competency. But you can achieve success with adequate effort.

Step 4.1: Tips for Creating Content on Your Own:

First and foremost, do yourself a favour and learn the basics of the self-publishing business. You do not have to pay to learn self-publishing in the beginning. All you have to do is do some research on Google and the YouTube platform.

Here are some free and paid resources for learning about self-publishing businesses:

WEBSITES (Type self-publishing guide in the Google search bar and you will get plenty of sites and forums.):

- (Amazon-Free and Must Read) kdp.amazon.com
- self-publishingschool.com/
- thebookdesigner.com/
- thebalancecareers.com
- Udemy.com–Video Tutorials (Paid)
- nichehacks.com,
- incomeschool.com, etc

YouTube Channels:

- Keith Wheeler Books,
- Rachel Harrison-Sund
- Project Life Mastery:
- Paul Marles-Must See
- Kelli Roberts
- Self-Publishing School
- Self-Publishing with Dale–Must Follow
- Shashwat Ashiya – Must Follow
- StackinProfit, etc.

Free And Paid Tools for Creating the Resources:

- You can use the free version of Canva.com for creating the book cover, LCB, and NCB book interior (though the paid version is worth investing in).
- Microsoft PowerPoint or Google Slides for LCB and NCB books (free).
- Use Microsoft Word or Google Docs for creating HCB books (free).
- Photoshop and Illustrator for graphics design.
- For colouring book design, use drawing tablets from brands like XPen, IPad, Huion, etc.

Many of the Self-publishing YouTube channel admins run the courses on self-publishing. You can first watch their channel, and if you are convinced by their method of teaching, then you can opt for their paid courses for more details.

Note: I am not affiliated with any of these websites or YouTube channels. These are the channels that often helped me personally to develop my self-publishing skills, so out of my experience, I am suggesting you these things. But you are free to do your research.

Approach for Creating Content for LCB, NCB, and HCB

The approaches for creating content for LCB, NCB, and HCB differ a lot.

LCB and NCB Book Content Strategy:

LCB and NCB books can be created using simple graphics using tools as mentioned in previous sections.

You can also use pre-made graphics or content from websites like:

- creativefabrica.com
- vecteezy.com

- BookBolt.io
- Gumroad.com
- Canva.com
- TangentTemplets.com
- BookBird.com, etc.

Once the content is ready, you can use canva.com to create the cover.

HCB's Book Content Strategy:

Finalize the niche for your HCB and before writing your book, start by writing the book outline. You can write your book's content in Microsoft Word or Google Docs for free.

The book outline should include the following points:

- A brief book introduction and purpose
- book title, sub-title, description, word length, target audience.
- Table of Content (You can refer to the table of content from your competitor's books.)
- Body Chapters.
- This is the problem that your book is trying to address.
- How are you addressing that problem and providing a solution to that problem?
- How do you want to conclude the book?
- collection of resources from Google, YouTube, and another competitor's book. (You can paste links to those resources in the outline document for reference.)

Once the book outline is ready, you can start writing the book content as per the outline.

Remember the following points while writing book content:

- Do provide valuable and in-depth information.
- Write the content straight to the point and focused.
- Nothing bluff should be written.
- Organize the content in a logical order.
- Maintain the connectivity of the content.
- The language and word use must be grammatically correct, interesting, and keep the reader engaged until the end of the book.

Step-4.2: Outsourcing Book Content Work

You can have your HCB (print book, eBook, and audio book) book written or narrated by ghostwriters. And for LCB and NCB books, you can get it done by hiring graphics or content designers from freelancing websites.

Note: Ghostwriters are the ones who write the book on your behalf as per your guidelines.

Some websites for hiring the best ghostwriters and audio book narrators:

- Upwork.com - My Option
- Fiverr.com
- theurbanwriters.com
- hotghostwriter.com
- Freelancer.com
- PeoplePerHour.com, etc.

Some websites for hiring graphics designers and content designers:

- Upwork.com
- Fiverr.com: My Choice
- Freelancer.com, etc

Important points to remember before hiring a content writer and designer:

- Content writers do not know what you want, so you must clarify for them your needs and requirements.
- Give them a detailed book outline so that they can work efficiently.
- It will take time and experience for you to find and deal with good ghostwriters and designers.
- The nominal rate for a ghostwriter is $1.5 to $2 per 100 words. and around $15 to $50 for graphics design for low-content books.
- Sometimes people will cheat, and that's the fact. Do not accept the work done by ghost-writers and designers blindly. You have to verify that the content submitted by them is not copied and is relevant to the topic.
- If they need to use any copyrighted material, then make sure they use approved materials only, or you can purchase such materials and give them to use.
- Once the content is ready, you can proofread, edit, and format your book on your own.

Things that can be outsourced ideally:

- Book Content Design.
- process of keyword research.
- Cover Design.
- audiobook narration.

Step-5: Proofread, Edit, and Formatting of Book.

Once the book draft is ready, proofread the book for the correctness of the content.

You can verify the following points while proofreading the content:

- Verify that content is not copied from external sources.
- For the HCB Print version of the book, do a plagiarism check using tools like Grammarly, Duplichecker, siteliner, Copyscape, plgscan, plagiarisma, etc.
- For LCB and NCB books, verify that only licensed images and graphics are used.
- Check for grammatical mistakes and spelling errors. You can also use the Grammarly tool (Free and Paid) to catch the error that you may miss.
- Verify that content is designed or written as per the book outline.

Once Proofreading of the content is done, Edit and Format the Book.

- Edit the book content like Table of content, Headers, paragraph, font size, font type, letter space, etc.
- Format images and Image titles.
- Add footnotes, copyright labels, and page numbers.
- Add page break wherever necessary.
- Change book size as per requirement. Eg: 6x9, 8.5x11 inches, etc.
- Format the content in logical order.
- Edit the Title, and author name.
- Add book description, copyright page, and disclaimer information.

Audiobook editing and proofreading tips

- Verify the voice and voice quality.
- Verify the articulation of the content.
- Verify the tone and its suitability for the content and the character.
- Verify the pace of the voice.
- Voice length
- Pronunciation.
- Language neutrality, etc.

Once you are happy with proofreading and done with editing and formatting your book, it is time to publish your book on self-publishing platforms.

Step 6: It's Time to Put Your Book Out There.

Before you publish your book, make a checklist.

- Approved Self-publishing Account A list of all the accounts of self-publishing platforms where you want to publish your book.
- Select the appropriate book language.
- Finalize the title, sub-title, other keywords, and description and keep them ready.
- Book Cover – for Paperback, eBook, and Audiobook.
- Finalize Book Size, Paper Type, Cover Type, Paper Colour, and Print Type (Regular or Large Print).
- Convert the book to the printable format specified by the self-publishing platform.
- Finalize Author Name (Use your name or pen name).
- Select bleed vs no bleed (You should have done this in the book outline phase).
- price for your book (eBook, Paperback, and Audiobook).
- Finalize the category under which you want to publish your book.
- You can buy your own ISBN or you can use an ISBN provided by self-publishing platforms. (Normally, most self-publishers use ISBNs provided by self-publishing platforms).

You have to have a checklist before publishing your book. This way you will not miss any steps, and the checklist also helps you prepare data well in advance. Often, last-moment preparation creates erroneous data, which can severely impact your book performance.

As mentioned above, keep everything ready and then start publishing your book.

You can enter the data as requested from the self-publication platforms, and once everything is entered, you can preview the book, and once satisfied with the results, you can press "Publish."

Once you publish your book, you may have to wait till your book is reviewed and audited by self-publication platforms, and then it will be live. Normally, this process will take 2 to 10 hours, but sometimes it may take days. Again, it all depends on self-publishing platforms.

Note: Once you publish your book, you cannot edit and make changes to the book's title or sub-title. If you make any mistakes while entering these fields, then it will severely impact your book performance. So, think twice before entering these fields and make sure twice before pressing the publish button. Because, after such a mistake, the only way to correct the mistake is to take down the book and republish it again as a new book.

Step 7: Market Your Book to Increase Its Reach

Self-publishing platforms organically display your books to their customers when you publish them. For this, they depend on your book title, sub-title, supporting keywords, and targeting keywords used in the title.

How well you rank for such targeted keywords depends on the competition for those keywords. Many times, when you enter a very competitive niche like Habits, Gratitude Journal, etc. in such conditions, you may never outperform other best-selling books in that niche, which have been selling well for many years and have very good reviews.

Ranking your books organically in such competitive niches is very difficult in the beginning. That is why you have to resort to advertisements on self-publishing platforms to create visibility for your books on the front page. You can buy ad space on the first page for your targeted keywords, and that way you can create visibility for your book.

You have control only till you create visibility through ads. Buying that book is up to the customer. But you can influence customers' decisions by creating an attractive book cover, with good and relevant keywords in the title and sub-title, and by writing a good book introduction, etc.

It costs more money to advertise in a competitive niche as compared to a less competitive niche. As a result, beginners are advised to publish books in a less competitive micro-niche rather than a more competitive broader niche.

You can also market your books for more visibility through the following means:

- You can also host and share your book's link on websites, Facebook Pages, WhatsApp Groups, Instagram posts, etc., and that way you can redirect the traffic to your books hosted on self-publishing platforms to buy books.
- You can also advertise your book link through Google Ads, social media platform ads like Facebook Ads, LinkedIn Ads, Instagram Ads, etc., and you can place an advertisement on other websites for a commission-based sharing model.
- You can do email marketing and share the book link and invite subscribers to buy books, etc.

There can be dozens of other ways through which you can advertise your book and create more visibility.

The best marketing strategies to advertise your book on self-publishing platforms like Amazon are:

- Ads work on the concept of a CPC (Cost per click) based auction model. Where your book is competing for advertisement space in the search results for the targeted niche. The higher the competition in that niche, the higher the CPC for that targeted keyword.
- When you run ads for your book, your book will be advertised to the buyer in the ad space requested. When a buyer sees your ad, it will be called an impression. You will not be charged for the impression. When the buyer clicks on the ad to check your book, that is when you will be charged.

- You can run ads manually or you can run auto-ads. In manual ads, you have to select the keywords for which you want to run ads.
- In the case of auto ads, based on your targeted keywords, the system will only run ads for you.
- If you are a complete beginner and do not know how to run manual ads, I suggest you start with auto ads.
- You can begin with smaller budgets, such as $5 with a 0.2 dollar bid price. Your bid amount will decide the impression of your books on the buyer. You can gradually increase the bid amount by $0.05 per step till you get the book impression and intern sale.
- Create names for your ad campaign. It will help you track the performance of each campaign (like A/B Testing) and also help you manage ads when you run ads for many books.
- Kill your ad if it does not get you a sale even after spending a maximum of $1 (this amount depends on your commission per sale of your book). The rule of thumb is that, per $1 spent on ads, you should have recovered that money through the sale of your book.
- If it gets a sale, continue the ad.
- When you get sales from auto ads, you can start manual ads for that book. Manual ads need keywords to target. You can use keywords from your keyword research or you can get keywords from advertisement reports of auto ads that brought sales.
- If you do not get sales for keywords for which you are running ads even after spending $1, then remove that keyword and continue testing for other keywords.
- Try this for the rest of the shortlisted keywords.
- Do not run ads for irrelevant keywords. Because such ads will only create an impression and will not generate a sale.
- More impressions and less sales or no sales will reduce the relevancy score of your book (eventually it will drop your book sale, so be careful). The relevance score will decide the organic ranking of your book in search results. Relevancy scope is a

measure that decides how relevant your book is for the search term used by the buyer.

- Your end goal of running ads should be to increase your book's ranking in search results and bring it to the top position in organic search results. Once you achieve that, you can stop the ads.
- You can also test your marketing strategy by changing book prices from time to time to test the book sale.
- You can also change the book cover often to test the book's sale.
- You can also bundle similar books to increase book sales.

Step 8: Expand Your Self-Publishing Business.

Now that you've published your first book and you've marketed it as planned, what next? Well, wait for 3 to 6 months for the book to rank well and then expect a decent sale. This is the standard duration for any book to kick in sales organically.

Now that you know the process, what you need is to scale your publishing business from self-publishing on your own to a full-scale business that you can replicate, manage, and multiply.

Here are tips to help you grow from your first book to a full-scale business.

- You have only 24 hours. That means your productivity is strictly limited. And the only way to boost productivity is to outsource the work. Straight and simple.
- You can hire ghostwriters and graphic designers for your book. You can directly hire these writers or designers, or you can use websites like freelancer.com, fiverr.com, etc.
- Then create your business plan and work as per that.

- For task management, you can use business management tools like Microsoft to-do, Monday.com, etc.
- You can either do keyword research on your own or outsource it. You can also use paid tools like Helium, Keyword.io, etc.
- Amazon Advertising is the key to success in book publishing. So, experiment with many strategies and adopt the one that works and replicate that strategy in many other books.
- Create a book outline and repeat it for continuous success.
- Create a budget and allocate a budget for book creation, outsourcing, and advertising, etc.
- Build an email list.
- Diversify the business in multiple niches like NCB, LCB, and NCB.
- Protect the copyright and trademark of your book.
- You can even start your own publication and print your own books and books for others too.
- Invest in your own office and staff for long-term success and sustainability.
- Build your own authority. You can even build multiple-author authority for many of your pen names.
- You can expand your self-publishing business by marketing your books offline or through your own book house (offline and online).
- You can market your books on multiple platforms like Facebook Ads, Google Ads, etc. for more sales and reach.
- Creating a website and a blog for your successful books can even increase your sales and income.
- You can also licence your HCB books, especially novels, stories, etc., for making movies, web series, etc.
- For better tax management, create a company like an LLP and manage the publishing business through that.
- You can diversify your business into other domains like Print on Demand, Drop Shipping, Blogging, etc. to create multiple sources of income.

CHAPTER ELEVEN

Important Tips to Succeed in the Self-Publishing Business

Tip #1: To stay ahead of the competition, be unique and original.

The biggest advantage and problem with the self-publishing business is that anyone with a good internet connection and a little bit of book publishing skill can enter this business. And this created huge competition.

To stand out among the crowd, you are left with no choice but to create content that is unique, original, competitive, and of high quality.

Do not copy content from other books, but you can refer to other successful books for inspiration for your book.

Tips #2: Copyright and Trademark Protection:

Many people in the self-publishing business copy the content straight from other books, or from public domains, or from any other unauthorised sources to save money and for quick success.

Because of this, many of your original designs may also be copied by others. This not only affects your book sales but also drastically hits your income. As a result, you must keep an eye out for such things and take action whenever possible to protect your book and your creativity.

Tip #3: Perform keyword research.

Because of the huge influx of new publishers in the self-publishing business, almost all niches are overcrowded. So, to succeed in self-publishing, you have to be very good at keyword research.

Keyword research will help you find the right niche that is less crowded but highly profitable.

Tip #4: Adhere to the Self-publishing Platform Guidelines.

Your success completely depends on how well you follow the guidelines of self-publishing platforms. This can immediately make or break your business and can impact your passive income dream through book publishing.

So, take the time to understand their guidelines before you publish your first book.

Tips #5: Author Authority (Branding)

Building author authority gives not only credibility to your books but also helps you increase book sales. Author Authority is also a sign of book quality.

Author authority also helps you sell your book offline.

Tip #6: Create a Plan of Action:

Anyone can have accidental success in any field. But, for consistent and repeated success, you need a systematic action plan.

Self-publishing is a full-scale business. Whether you publish one book or 1,000, it must have a plan. Many times, beginners treat this business like a hobby and end up with no sales or even losing their account for wrong publishing practices.

If you want to make some serious money and want to generate passive income, then I suggest you have an action plan.

Your Action Plan should include:

- Keyword Research Strategy
- Daily, Weekly, Monthly, and Yearly Book Publishing Plans
- publishing guidelines.
- finance management plan.
- Taxation.
- Growth Strategies
- team building.
- marketing plan, etc.

Tips #7: Quality is Everything:

Because of overcrowding and neck-to-neck competition in the self-publishing business, the success window for beginners is very small.

There was a time when even low-quality books used to make good sales because of the lack of books in that niche. But now that is not the case. You will find thousands of books published in thousands of niches. So, to compete with such books, you may have to go one mile extra and create books that are unique and of the highest quality.

To create quality books, you may have to outsource your ideas to highly qualified designers or writers.

If you do not have much budget for such outsourcing, then I suggest you get proper training before you create your first piece of content.

Tips #8: Time, commitment, and patience are the keys:

Success in any field takes time. Self-publishing is not a get-rich-quick scheme. It is a business and a business will take time to reflect on the result. It is estimated that, on average, you may have to wait 6 to 12 months for a decent sale and sometimes even more.

That is why you have to have patience. In the self-publishing business, patience is the key. Those who are ready to wait will get the fruits of their work, and the rest will fade away.

Also, self-publishing is a continuous process. As time and demand change, your books will eventually fade away. That is why you have to be continuously creating and uploading books. This needs long-term commitment and discipline.

Do not lose hope during the beginning. At least for one year, commit to yourself that you will only create quality content in all possible niches and you will not expect anything from the self-publishing business. Trust me, eventually, you will start to see the results.

Remember, to produce quality books at the beginning, you have to take your focus off of money.

Tips #9: Focus on One Niche at a Time:

There are thousands of niches in book publishing, and you cannot begin publishing in all of them at the same time.

That is why you have to do keyword research and finalise some niches that have high potential, and out of those, pick any one of the niches and start publishing books in that.

I'm sure you're excited about publishing in multiple niches at once.Calm down. Practically, that is not possible. So, have patience and take one step at a time and target one niche at a time.

Because, while publishing, you will be learning many different things, and you will also be making many mistakes. So, when you take a step-by-step approach, you will get the opportunity to learn and correct your mistakes while you keep on publishing books.

Tips #10: Author Name Strategies:

Many beginners get confused while selecting the author's name. They do not know whether to select their original name as their author name or to select any pen name or any business name.

Do not worry, it happens to everyone. But here is the simple approach you can adopt.

Author names can be divided into 3 categories:

- Original author's name.
- Pen Name – Individual
- Pen Name – Business.

I suggest you use pen names for LCB and NCB books. Since NCB and LCB are often printed and published by organisations or publications rather than individuals, you can use business or publication pen names like ABC Publications, ABC Printers, etc. But you can also use any random individual pen name and there is nothing wrong with that.

The advantage of using business pen names is that, with the success of LCB and NCB, you can eventually convert that business name into a full-scale publication.

For HCB, it is advised to use the author's name only (pen name or your original name) rather than any business name. For self-help, it makes sense to use your original name, and for books like novels and stories, use a pen name.

- Use a penname when you do not like to identify yourself and you only want to make money rather than popularity.
- Use your original name if you want both popularity and money. Many authors use their original names because they want more popularity than money, and they would like to recognise themselves with their book. In particular, public speakers, professors, teachers, intellectuals, politicians, film stars, etc. prefer original names over pen names.
- Original author names also provide authority for books as well as confidence in buyers, especially in niches like health and fitness, self-help, etc.
- You should also be careful when using a pen name. Do not use pen names of famous publications or authors. Your pen name should be unique and free from copyright and trademark claims.
- Please read the self-publication platform guidelines before selecting the pen names. Because the wrong choice of a pen name can create problems like copyright claims and even block your account permanently if you repeat such mistakes.

CHAPTER TWELVE

Common Self-Publishing Mistakes and Tips to Avoid them

Keyword Stuffing in the Title, Sub-Title, Author Name, Pennames, etc.

- An unnatural number of keywords will create a misleading customer experience, which can damage the reputation of your books as well as impact the reputation of the self-publishing platforms.
- What you can do is use only 1 to 2 keywords in the title and sub-title. And use the rest of the keywords in the dedicated keyword entry section.
- Stuffing keywords in pennames and author names is strictly against the guidelines of self-publishing platforms.

Irrelevant keywords in the title, sub-title, keyword section, etc.

- Irrelevant keywords mislead customers and make them buy the wrong products. which is a strictly prohibited activity in the self-publishing business.
- You will not only lose business because of bad reviews and ratings, but you will also be restricted or banned from using these platforms for such activity.

Adding your books to the irrelevant category.

- Again, this creates a misleading customer experience and a bad reputation for your books and these platforms.
- Categories are meant to help people filter the right niche for them to search for their interesting books quickly and easily. Any cross-category can cast serious doubt on the self-publishing platform's filtering process, eventually driving customers away from these platforms due to poor customer service.
- An example of such an activity is adding a cooking book to the "Self-help" category.

One-to-one copy of the content, title, and sub-title from other books:

- It is OK if we take a reference from other successful competitors' books in our niche for inspiration and content ideas, but when you start copying their content as it is, you trigger not only bad customer reviews but also copyright infringement.
- Self-publishing platforms expect their showcase to contain multiple books with unique content so that customers can have many options for buying the product they are interested in.
- Copying the content is an offense. You may be fined or sued under the copyright and trademark infringement acts, and also,

you may end up giving all the money earned through that book and even lose your self-publishing account too. So, please stay away from it.

- You should maintain uniqueness in the title, sub-title, author name, and penname.
- Unknowingly or knowingly, many times we tend to use keywords or phrases or terms (e.g., Fortnite, Pokémon, Instant Pot, etc.) which are copyrighted and we may use images or graphics which may be trademarked. To be on the safe side, always double-check on copyright and trademark verification websites (a must in the United States and the United Kingdom).If such keywords, phrases, or graphics are already covered under a trademark or copyright, avoid using them. You can use only copyright-free and trademark-free materials for self-publishing businesses, or you can purchase a licence for the same.
- You can also buy the licence for such images, graphics, or keywords and phrases from the creators and then use them in your book.

Do not maintain multiple self-publishing accounts under the same name.

- As per self-publishing guidelines, you must maintain only one publishing account under one entity. That's it. It is OK to have one publishing account under your name, one under your company, and/or multiple companies. Unless you create one account per entity, you are fine.
- Again, please read and crosscheck the guidelines and rules for creating multiple accounts.

Grammatical mistakes

The biggest problem with beginners is grammatical mistakes. Many countries other than English-speaking countries are poor at framing English books because of grammatical mistakes.

Grammar mistakes can ruin your business in the long run. People often leave poor reviews and ratings for your books, which in turn will hit your sales and ranking.

Tips to correct grammar mistakes

- You can outsource your book to a ghost writer or designer.
- You can use tools like Grammarly (paid version) to correct your grammatical mistakes.
- You can outsource proofreading to correct grammatical mistakes.

Wrong Niche selection

Self-publishing any book is a long process. From keyword research to publishing a book, it can take up to a month or more. So, it becomes very important for you to select the right niche before you create your book, or else you will lose time as well as your efforts, and in return, you will get nothing.

Copyright and Trademark Infringement:

Please do not copy content from other websites or books as it is. I know some of you may be thinking of a shortcut to make money by copying the content of other books or websites as it is.

But this business will not work like that. Self-publishing platforms consider copyright and trademark infringement as serious crimes, and they not only block your earnings but can also permanently block you from publishing books.

The shortcut may sound easy and exciting, but it is not a sustainable solution. If you want to generate passive income, then consider this business seriously and respect and follow all the dimensions of publishing.

Publishing Speed

Did you know? Every day, thousands of people are adding thousands of books in thousands of niches. Some people even upload more than 50 books a day.

If you ever want to compete with their books and make money, then you must be fast enough to publish your books. We are in the information age and any delay in time to market can cost you thousands of dollars in profit.

Tips to Increase the Speed of Publishing Books:

- Commit to the business and cultivate the discipline to follow through on that commitment.
- Have a clear and achievable action plan.
- Stop wasting time.
- Do not re-invent the wheel; buy the resources and interiors wherever needed.
- Wherever possible, outsource the work.
- And finally, do not compromise quality for the sake of speed. Rather, maintain the balance between the two.

Pricing your book - Proper Pricing Method:

- Book pricing is also an important factor in the success of your book. Do not overcharge or undercharge your book.

- Refer to your competition and charge your book around that price, or a better approach is to charge the average of 10 bestselling book prices in your niche.
- You can even experiment with book pricing and stick to the one where you get the maximum sales as well as profit.
- Remember, charging too low will not guarantee the sale of your book. Sometimes, people do not prefer to buy books that are priced too low, and charging low can even give the impression of a lower quality book.

Trying to Save Money where you are supposed to Invest:

- If you have money to invest, then please invest the money in buying tools and resources like graphics, etc. You can even use the money to outsource the book design.
- If you are confident in your ability to design a book, then it is perfectly fine to design your book yourself. Else, it's better to outsource it. Because low-quality books will never bring you any sales.

CHAPTER THIRTEEN

What Next?

Now that you have understood the entire process of self-publishing your first book, do not waste any more time. Get up and start the publishing process.

We often become victims of analysis paralysis and we never initiate the action to create the book.

The best thing to do before starting any business is not to think of the result. What I suggest to you is to do some basic keyword research, finalise one niche, and straight away start creating the book. Do not worry much about quality in the beginning; first finish the book and make it live.

Once you have done this, you will understand the entire self-publishing process. From then on, start doing proper research and then take your time and create quality books.

So, do not wait much; go ahead and take your first step.

CHAPTER FOURTEEN

A Note of Thanks

Thanks for considering this book among others. I've tried to provide as much information as possible.

All my efforts will be effective only when you take action and create a successful passive income for yourself.

Thanks for sticking up here.

I wish you the best of luck with your business.

Thanks, and regards.

9 798888 497623

Printed by Libri Plureos GmbH in Hamburg,
Germany